Green Day
nimrod.

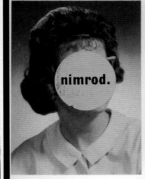

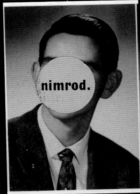

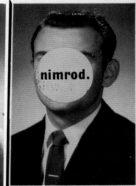

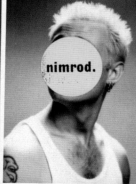

Transcribed by KENN CHIPKIN
Project Manager: Aaron Stang
Music Editor: Colgan Bryan
CD Art Direction and Design: Chris Bilheimer
Photography: Snorri Brothers and Chris Bilheimer
Book Layout: Odalis Soto

WARNER BROS. PUBLICATIONS - THE GLOBAL LEADER IN PRINT
USA: 15800 NW 48th Avenue, Miami, FL 33014

WARNER/CHAPPELL MUSIC

Carisch
NUOVA CARISCH

IMP
INTERNATIONAL MUSIC PUBLICATIONS LIMITED

CANADA: 85 SCARSDALE ROAD, SUITE 101
DON MILLS, ONTARIO, M3B 2R2
SCANDINAVIA: P.O. BOX 533, VENDEVAGEN 85 B
S-182 15, DANDERYD, SWEDEN
AUSTRALIA: P.O. BOX 353
3 TALAVERA ROAD, NORTH RYDE N.S.W. 2113

ITALY: VIA CAMPANIA, 12
20098 S. GIULIANO MILANESE (MI)
ZONA INDUSTRIALE SESTO ULTERIANO
SPAIN: MAGALLANES, 25
28015 MADRID
FRANCE: 25 RUE DE HAUTEVILLE, 75010 PARIS

ENGLAND: SOUTHEND ROAD,
WOODFORD GREEN, ESSEX IG8 8HN
GERMANY: MARSTALLSTR. 8, D-80539 MUNCHEN
DENMARK: DANMUSIK, VOGNMAGERGADE 7
DK 1120 KOBENHAVNK

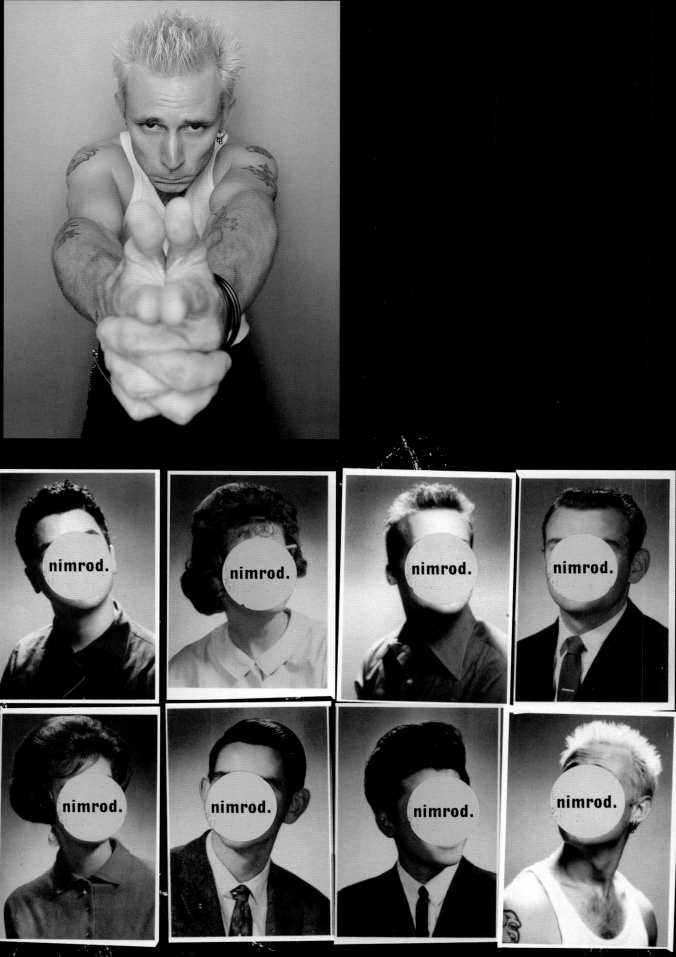

million; the menders also to   ish a   wen
th $ 000.
The Bo ton area co tinu d tc be   ured
  holdups. Six in   months, includin   ne in   ncy
A   l and on   ockt   n   y h   ght the tota
  t from major   mes in east   ts since
  0 to nearly   lion.
The
  nvic   w
  n mid-1
  ause of a   o
   pri onment   bbery
sa t, and   ners h
  ped fr   on Fe   y 24 an
as recaptu   the next day wi

Contents

NICE GUYS FINISH LAST

Lyrics by BILLIE JOE
Music by BILLIE JOE and GREEN DAY

8

Pre-Chorus:

Pres - sure cook - er, pick___ my brain___ and___

tell me I'm in - sane.___ I'm so fuck - ing hap-

py, I___ could___ cry.___ Ev - 'ry joke can have_

___ its truth,___ but___ now the joke's on you.___ I

nev - er knew you're such___ a fun - ny___ guy.

Chorus:

Oh,___ nice guys fin - ish last,___ when

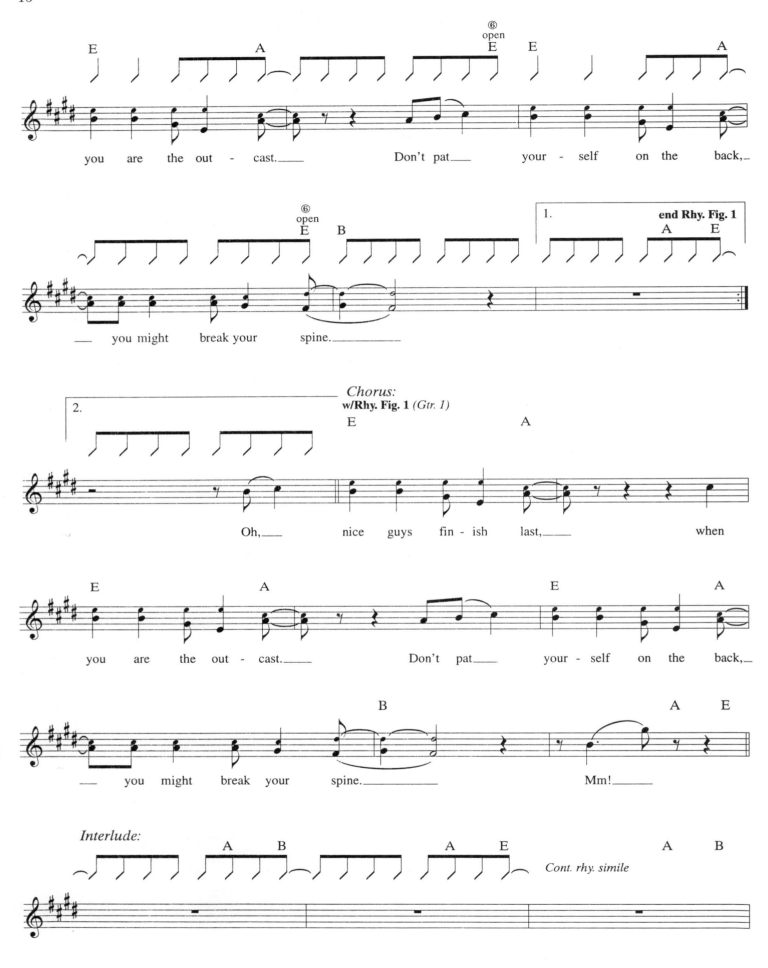

HITCHIN' A RIDE

Lyrics by BILLIE JOE
Music by BILLIE JOE and GREEN DAY

*Play only lowest two notes of chord when P.M. is indicated (throughout).

1. Hey, mis - ter, where you head - ed? Are you in a hur - ry?
2. Cold tur - key's get - ting stale, to - night I'm eat - ing crow.

ry? I need a lift to hap - py hour, say, oh no.
Fer - ment - ed sal - mo - nel - la, poi - son oak, no.

Hitchin' a Ride - 6 - 1
0224B

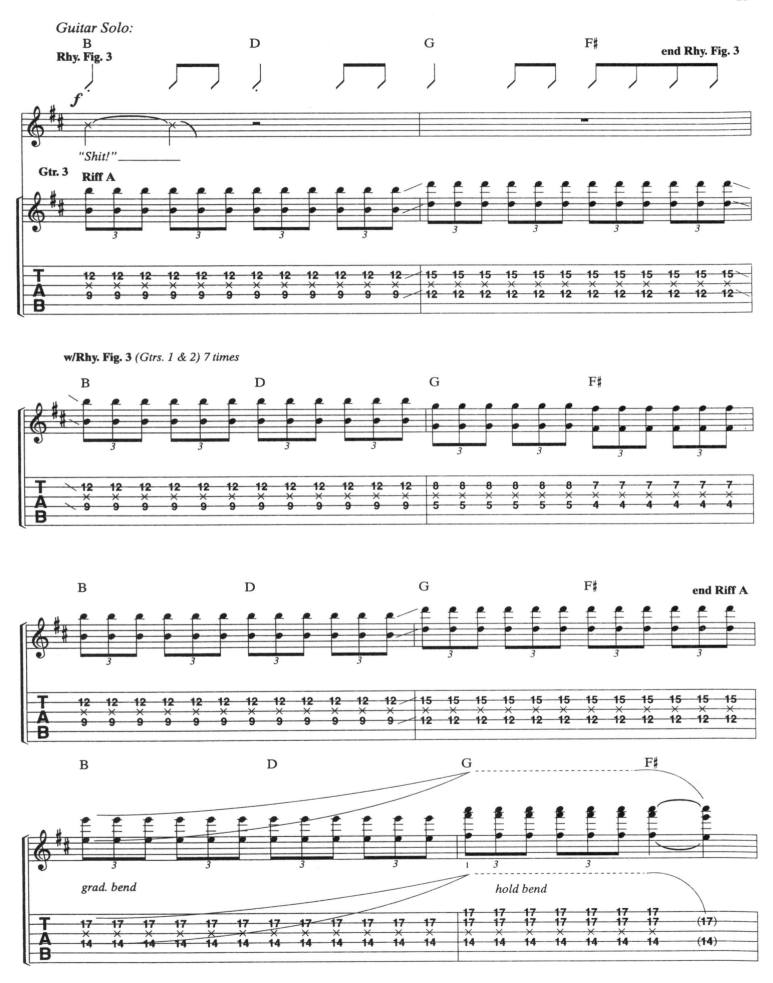

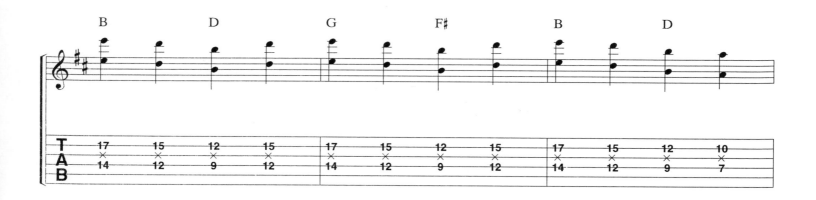

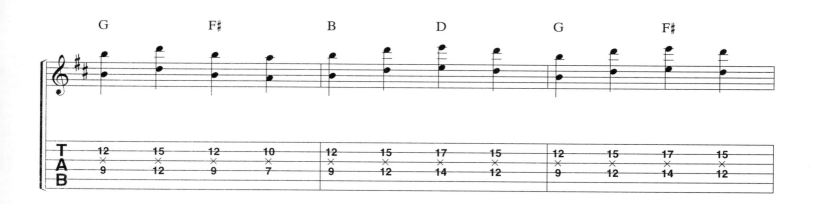

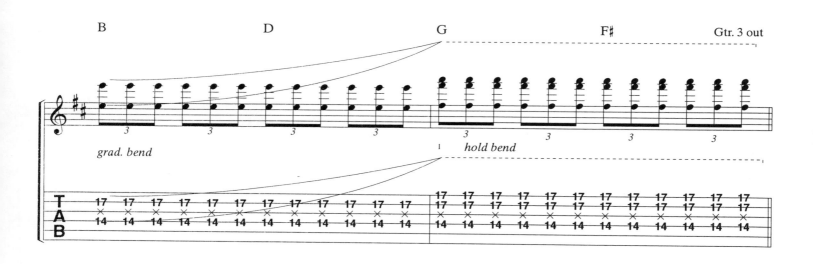

Chorus:
w/Rhy. Fig. 2 *(Gtrs. 1 & 2)*

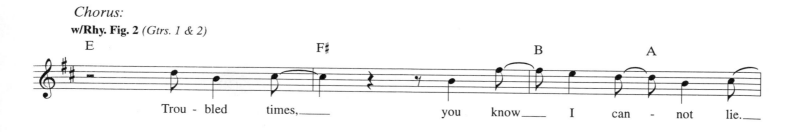

Trou - bled times,____ you know____ I can - not lie.____

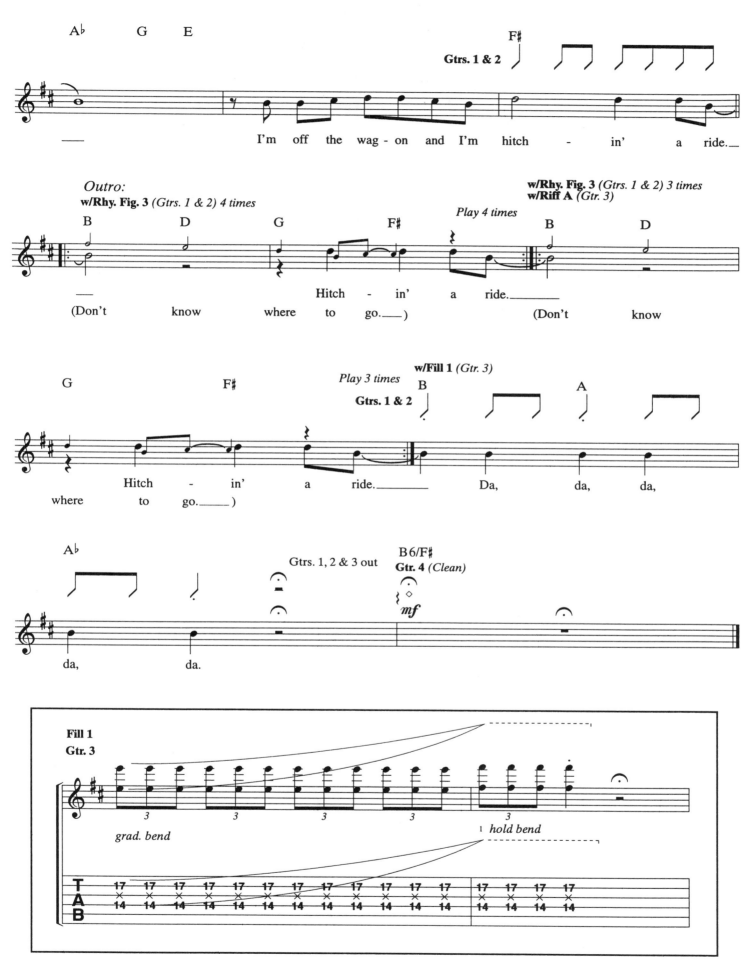

THE GROUCH

Lyrics by BILLIE JOE
Music by BILLIE JOE and GREEN DAY

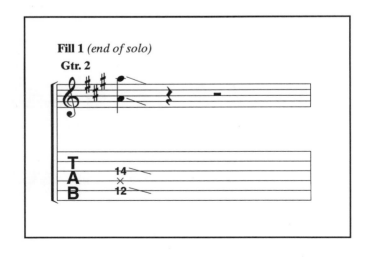

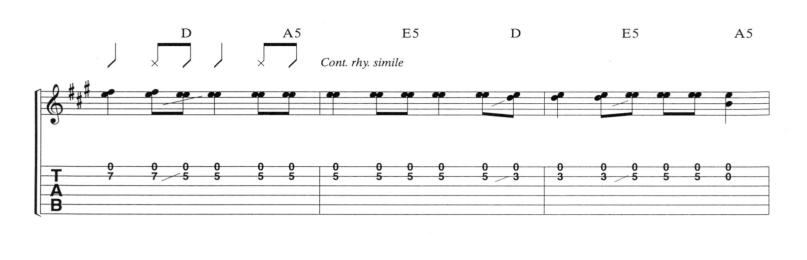

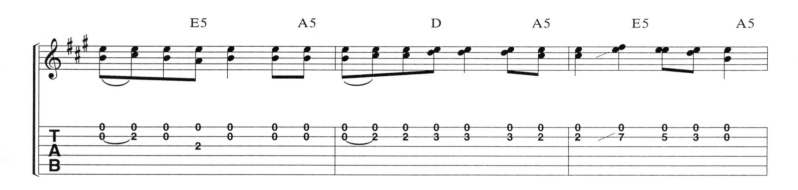

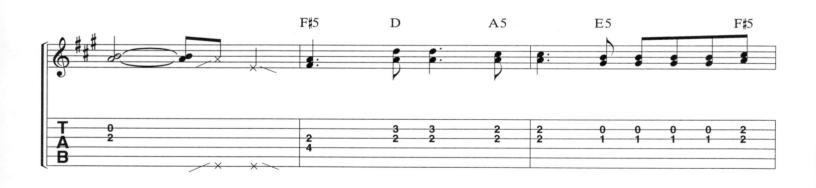

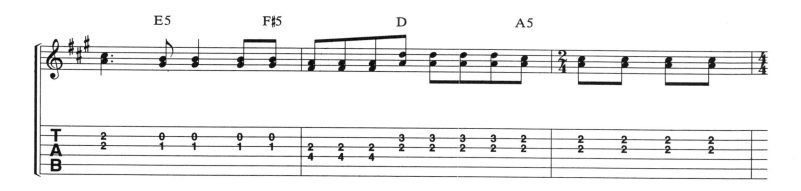

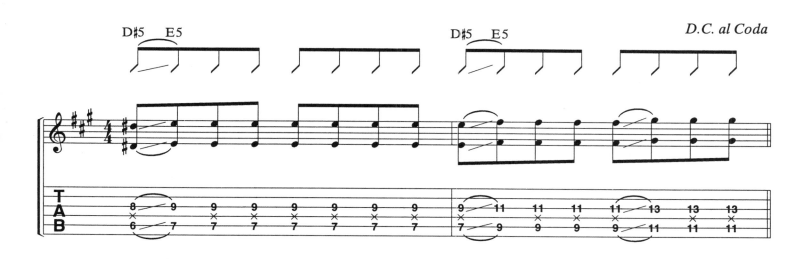

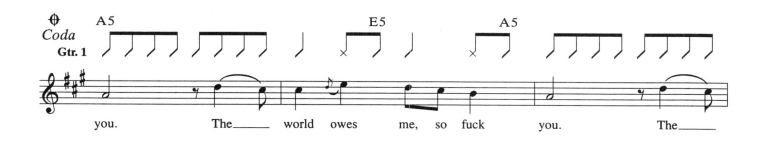

you. The_____ world owes me, so fuck you. The_____

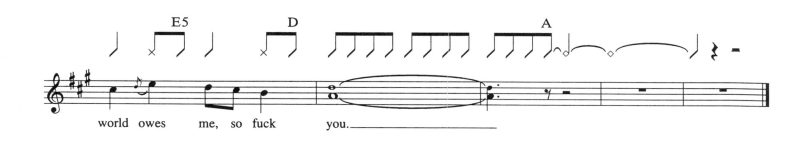

world owes me, so fuck you._____

REDUNDANT

Lyrics by BILLIE JOE
Music by BILLIE JOE and GREEN DAY

Chorus:

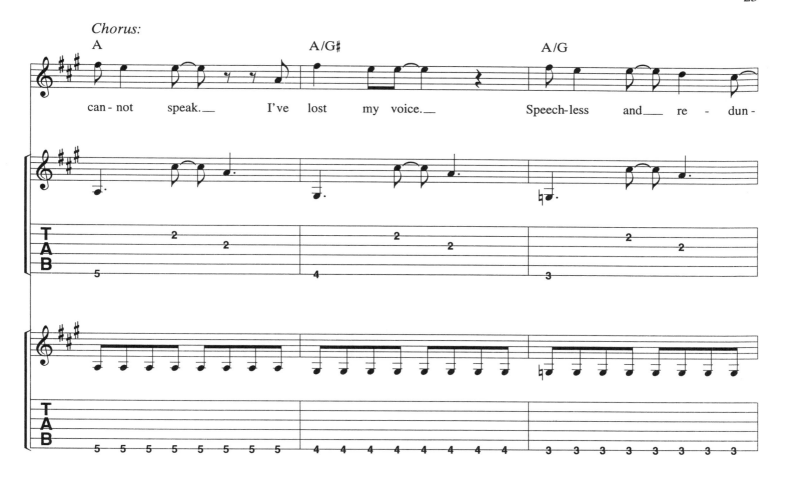

can - not speak.__ I've lost my voice.__ Speech-less and__ re - dun -

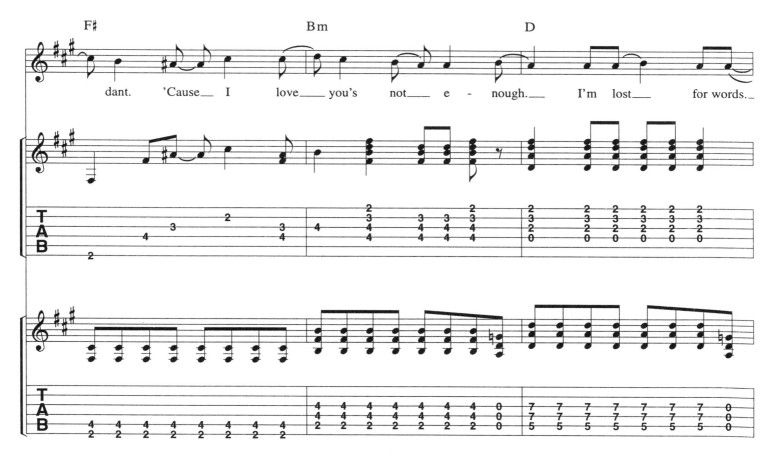

dant. 'Cause__ I love__ you's not__ e - nough.__ I'm lost__ for words.__

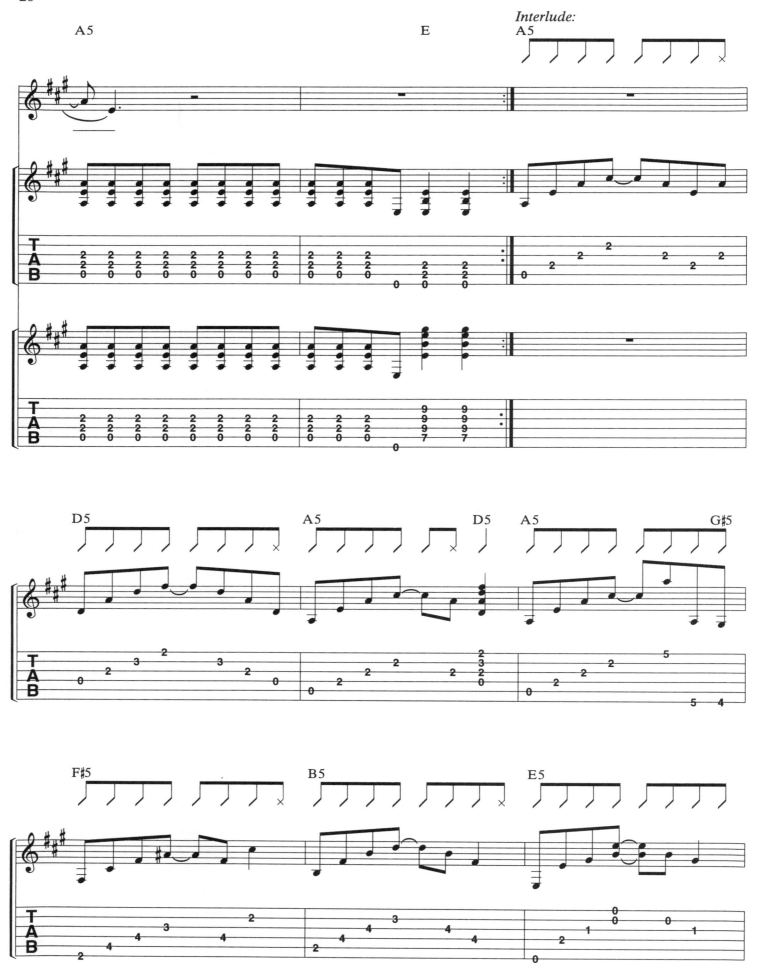

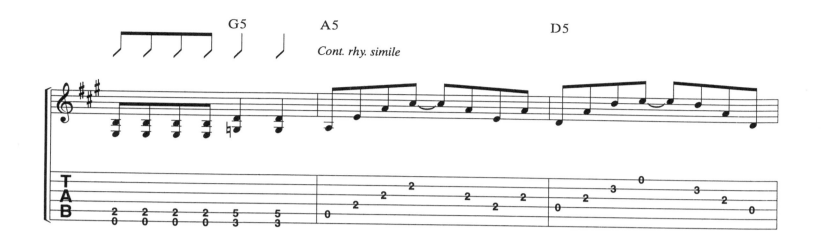

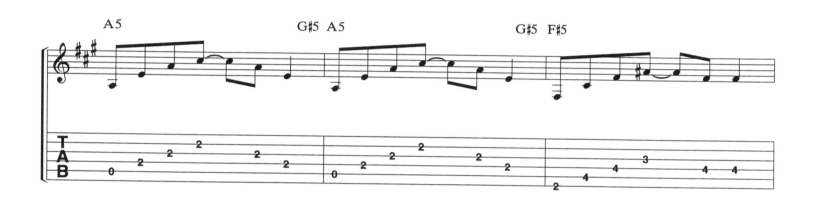

Now I

Chorus:

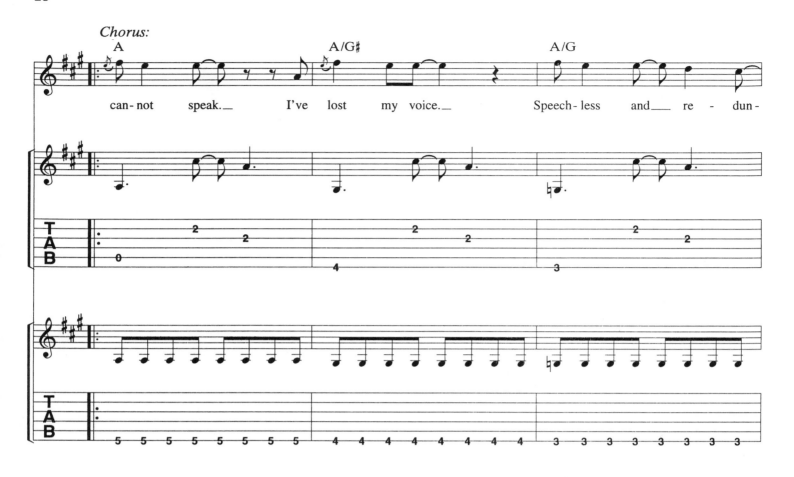

can-not speak.__ I've lost my voice.__ Speech-less and__ re-dun-

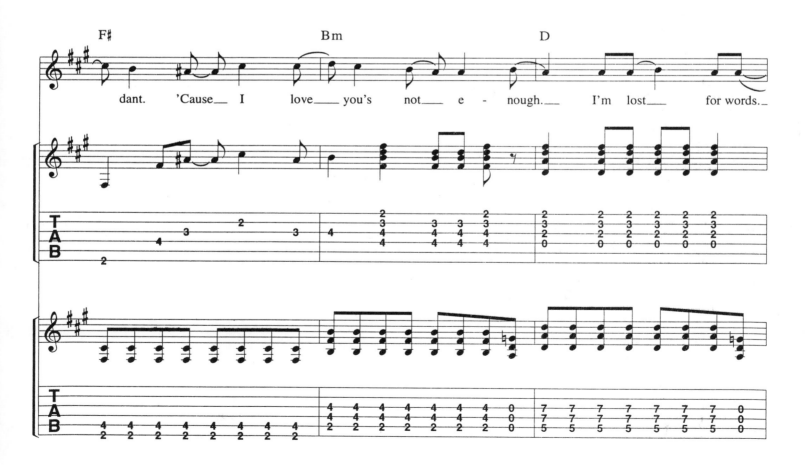

dant. 'Cause__ I love__ you's not__ e-nough.__ I'm lost__ for words.__

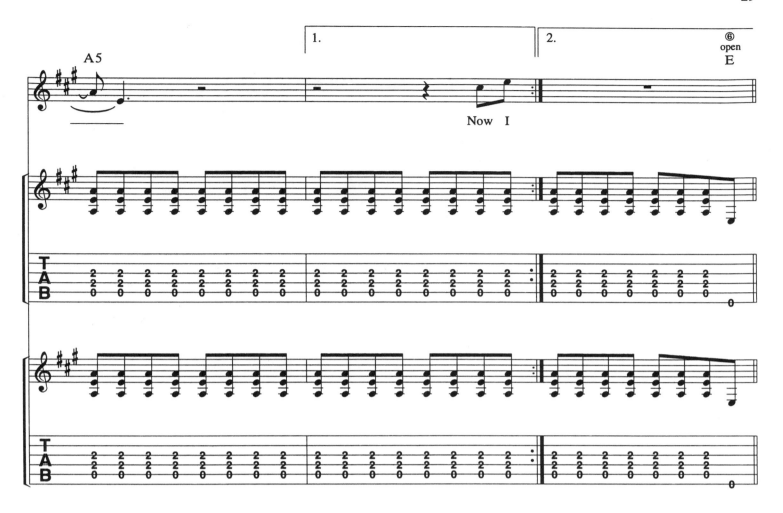

Now I

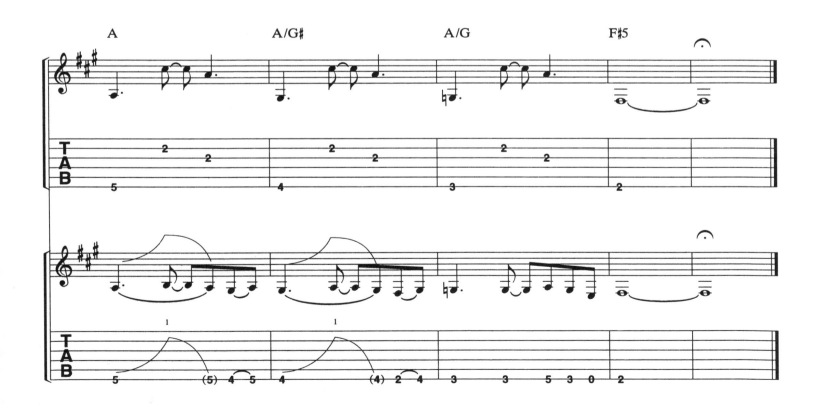

SCATTERED

Lyrics by BILLIE JOE
Music by BILLIE JOE and GREEN DAY

Makes me wish that you___ were___ here.___ 'Cause now it seems__ I've for-
Lodged to fill an - oth - er___ year.___ Well, drag it on___ and on__

got - ten___ my pur - pose in___ this life._____ Well,
— un - til___ my skin is ripped___ to shreds._____ I'm

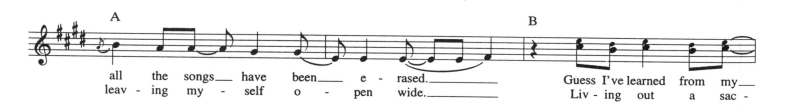

all the songs___ have been___ e - rased._____ Guess I've learned from my___
leav - ing my - self o - pen wide._____ Liv - ing out a sac -

%*Chorus:*

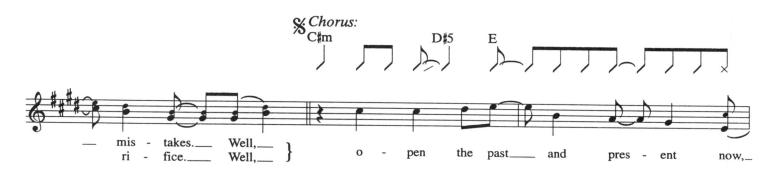

— mis - takes.___ Well,___
ri - fice.___ Well,___ } o - pen the past___ and pres - ent now,__

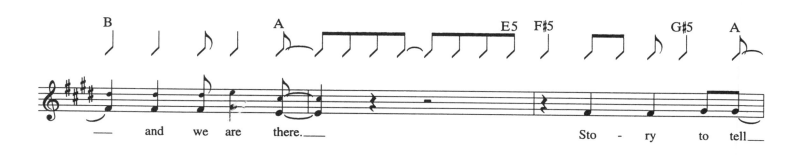

— and we are there.___ Sto - ry to tell___

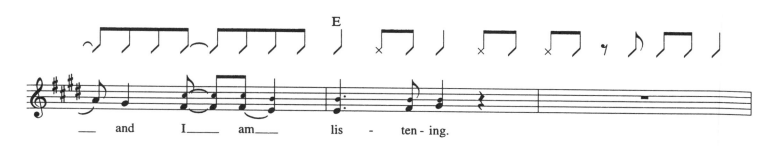

— and I___ am___ lis - ten - ing.

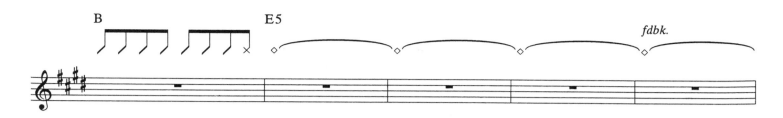

Verse 3:

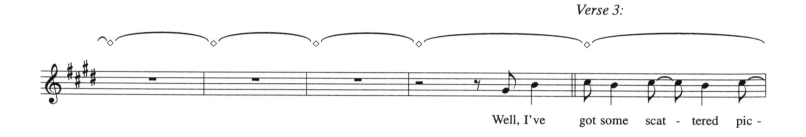

Well, I've got some scat - tered pic -

tures ly - ing on___ my bed - room floor.___ It re -

*Implied by Bass gtr.

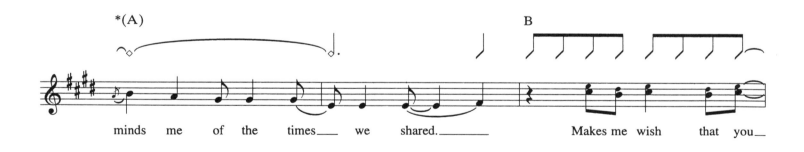

minds me of the times___ we shared.____ Makes me wish that you___

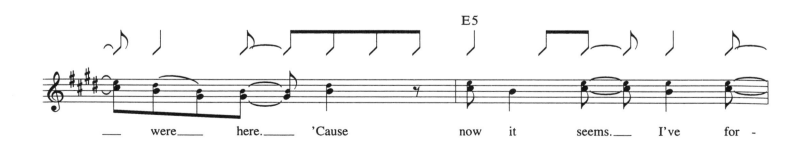

___ were___ here.___ 'Cause now it seems.___ I've for -

Scattered - 5 - 4
0224B

WORRY ROCK

Lyrics by BILLIE JOE
Music by BILLIE JOE and GREEN DAY

36

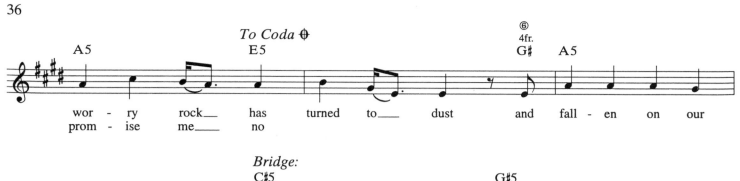

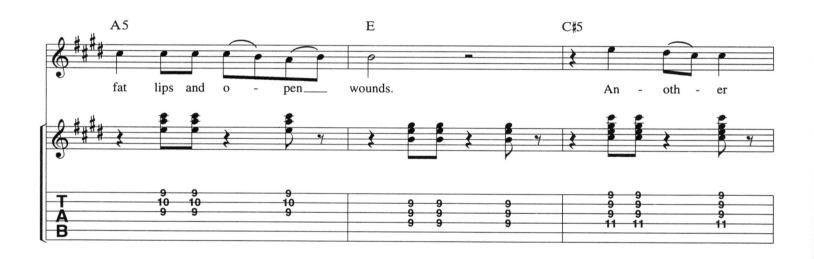

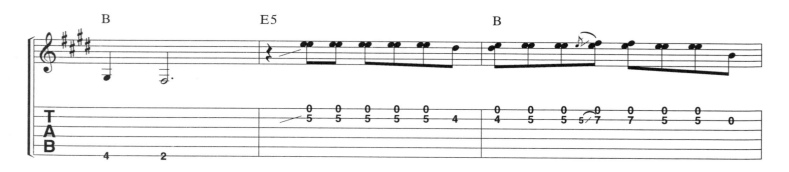

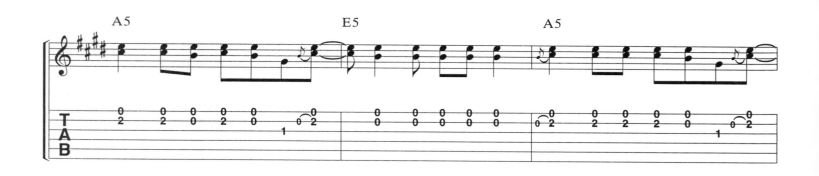

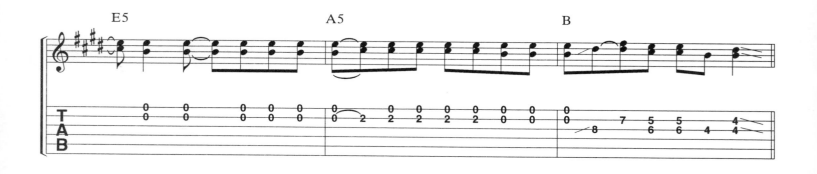

Bridge:
w/Rhy. Fig. 1 *(Gtr. 2) simile*

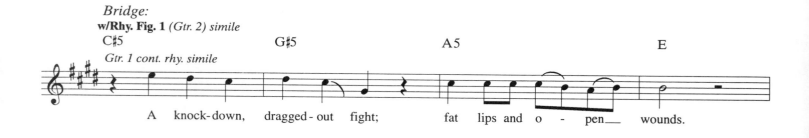

A knock-down, dragged-out fight; fat lips and o - pen___ wounds.

D. C. al Coda

An - oth - er wast - ed night, and no one will take___ the___ fall.

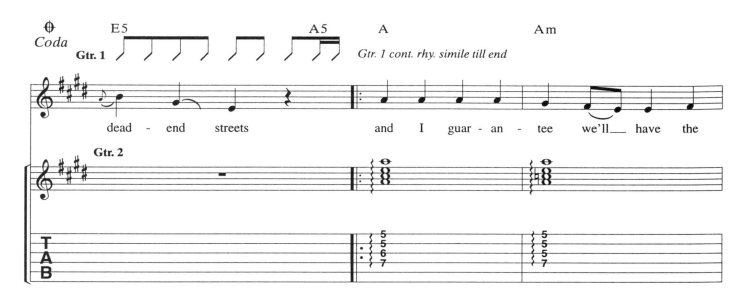

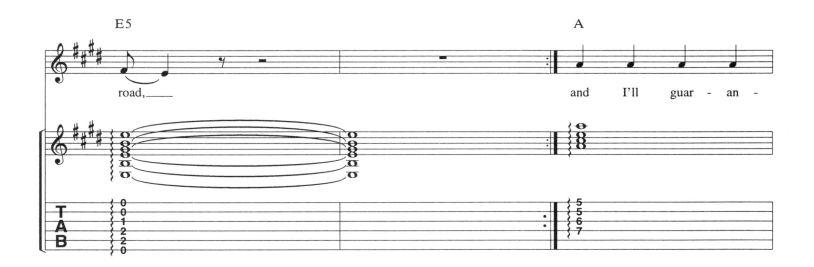

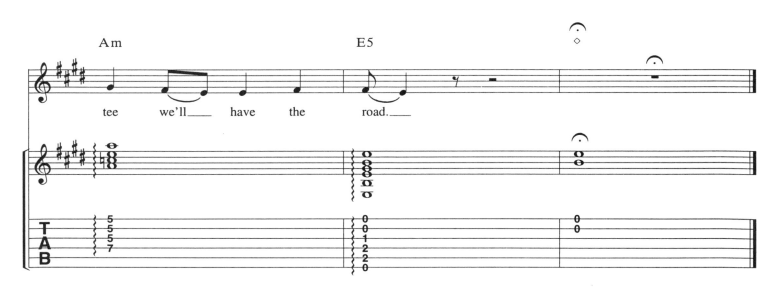

Worry Rock - 5 - 5
0224B

ALL THE TIME

Lyrics by BILLIE JOE
Music by BILLIE JOE and GREEN DAY

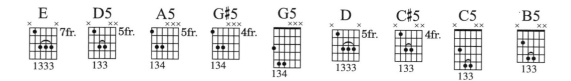

Moderately fast ♩ = 160

Intro:

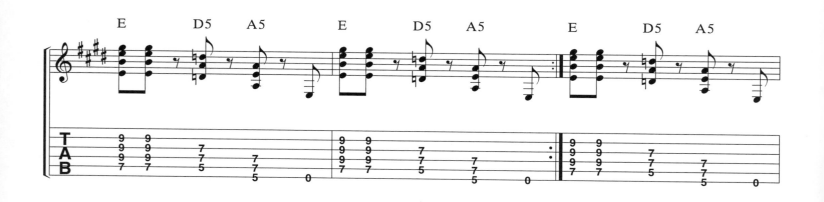

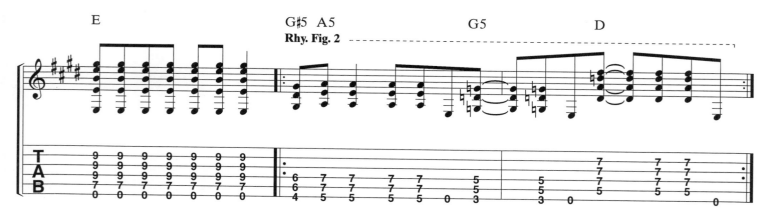

All the Time - 4 - 1
0224B

Chorus:

All the time, ev - 'ry - time I need it.____ What's the time? I'd say the

time is right. Here's to me. Let's find____ an - oth - er rea - son.____

Down the hatch and a bad at - ti - tude. Sal - ud.____

𝄋 Verse:

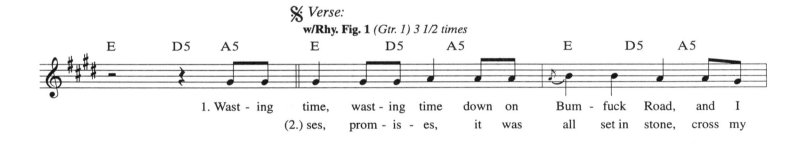

1. Wast - ing time, wast - ing time down on Bum - fuck Road, and I
(2.) ses, prom - is - es, it was all set in stone, cross my

don't know where the hell it - 'll go._____ Heir - loom and huff - ing fumes, and I'm
heart and I hope to die._____ Sug - ar fix, dirt - y tricks and a

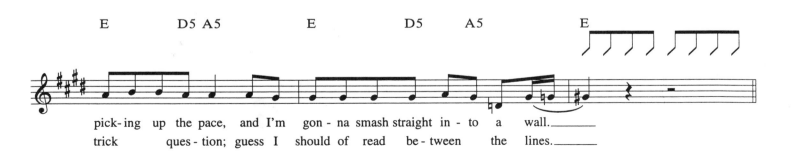

pick - ing up the pace, and I'm gon - na smash straight in - to a wall.____
trick ques - tion; guess I should of read be - tween the lines.____

42

All the Time - 4 - 3
0224B

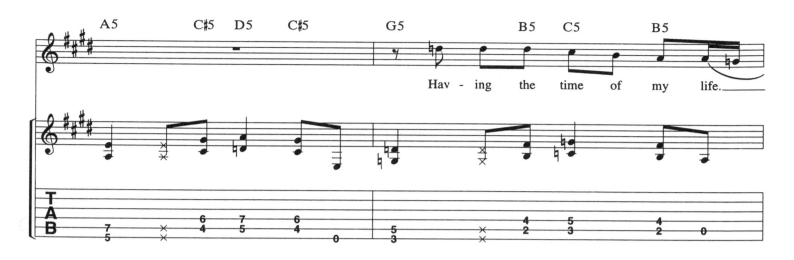

D. S. S. 𝄌𝄌 al Coda II

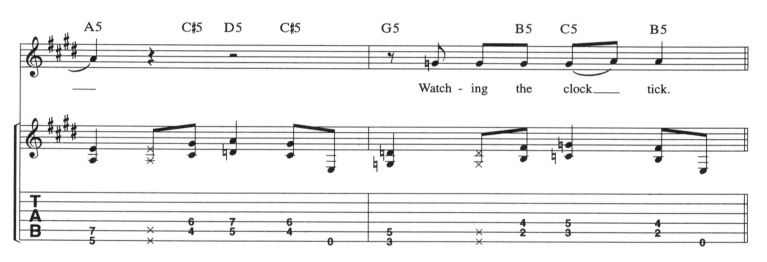

Coda II **w/Rhy. Fig. 1** *(Gtr. 1)*

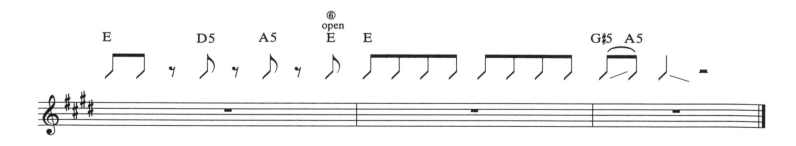

PLATYPUS (I HATE YOU)

Lyrics by BILLIE JOE
Music by BILLIE JOE and GREEN DAY

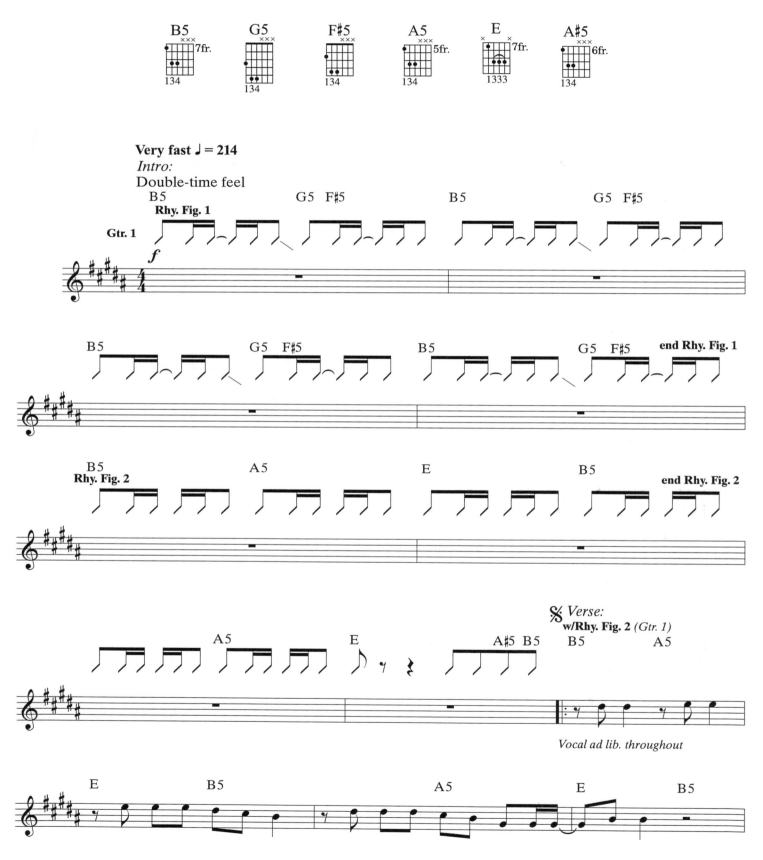

Vocal ad lib. throughout

Platypus (I Hate You) - 4 - 1
0224B

Pre-Chorus:

46

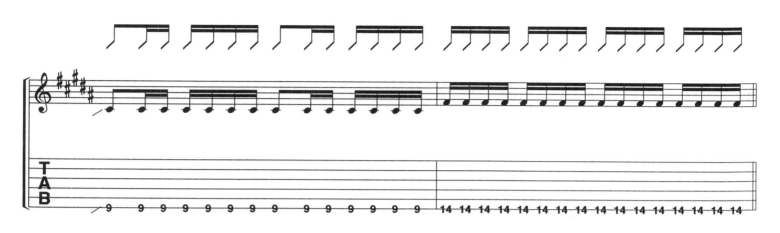

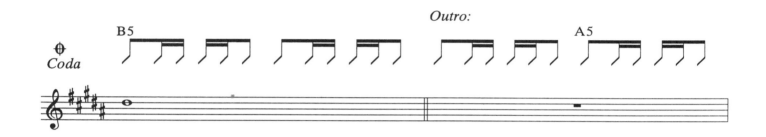

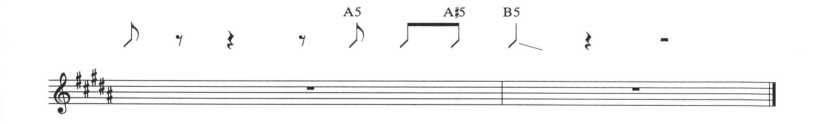

UPTIGHT

Lyrics by BILLIE JOE
Music by BILLIE JOE and GREEN DAY

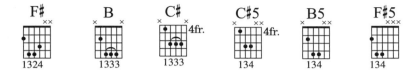

Moderately fast ♩ = 168

Intro:

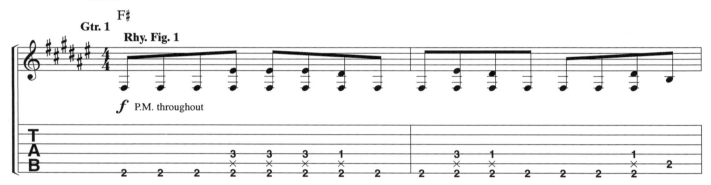

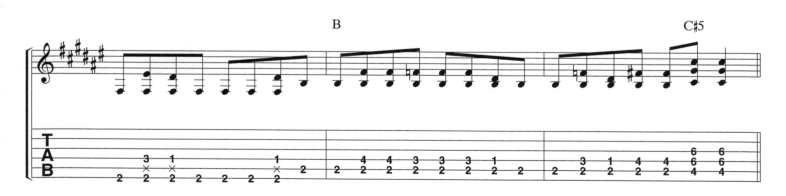

Uptight - 4 - 1
0224B

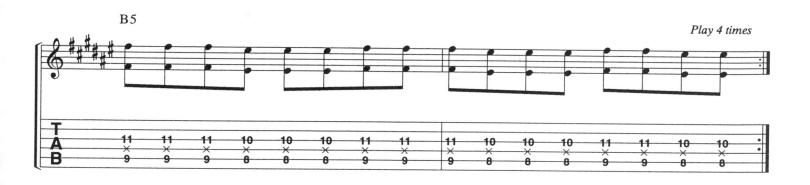

Play 4 times

Chorus:
w/Rhy. Fig. 2 *(Gtr. 1)*

Up - tight, I'm a nag___ with a gun,___ yeah. All night, su - i - cide's_

— last call.___ I've been up - tight, all___ night,___ I'm a son of a gun._

— Up - tight, I'm a nag___ with a gun,___ yeah.

All night, su - i - cide's___ last call.___ I've been up - tight, all___ night,_

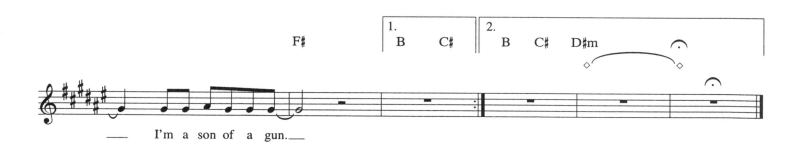

___ I'm a son of a gun.___

LAST RIDE IN

Lyrics by BILLIE JOE
Music by BILLIE JOE and GREEN DAY

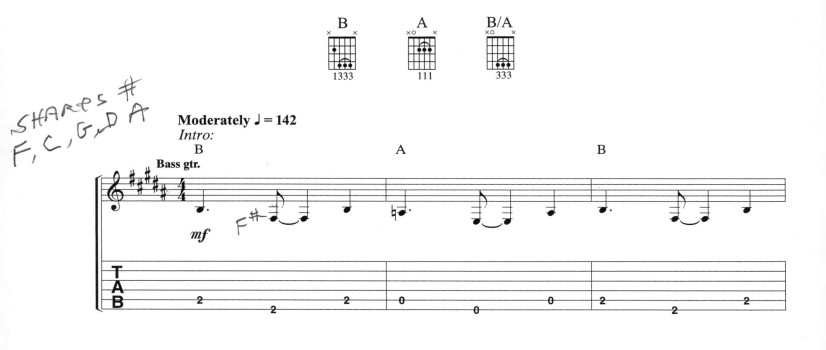

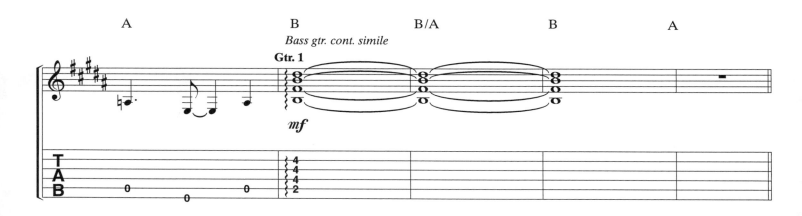

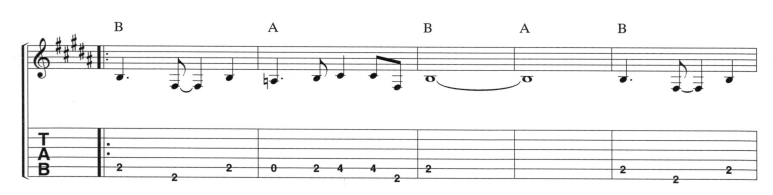

Last Ride In - 5 - 1
0224B

*Vibes ad lib. solo on repeat.

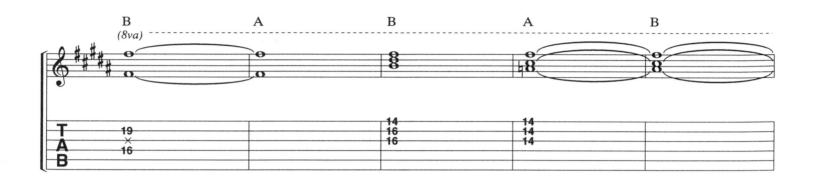

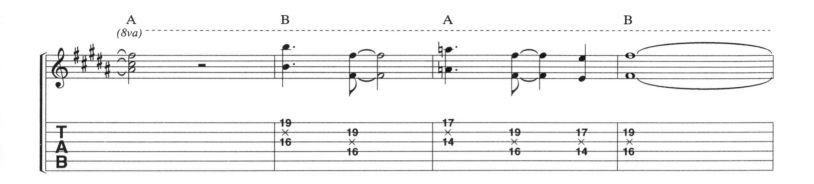

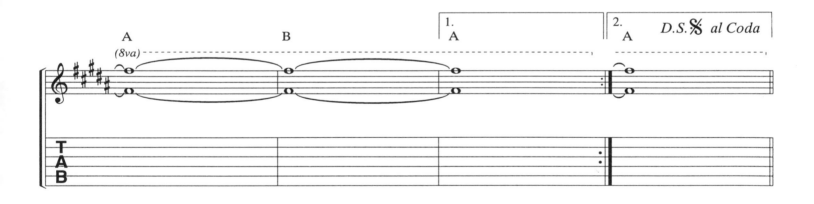

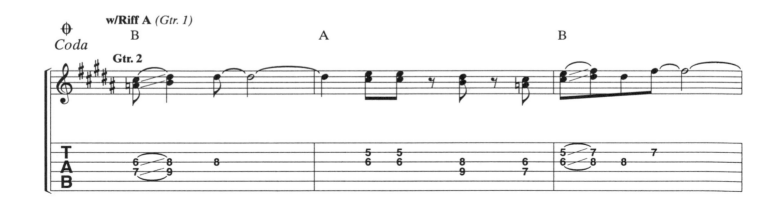

56

Gtr. 2 tacet

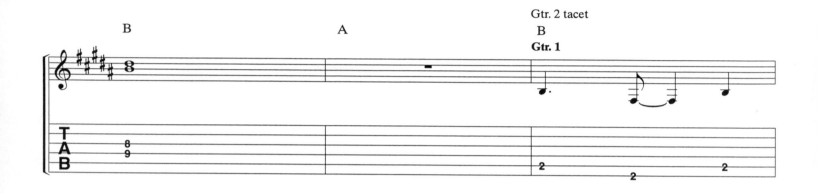

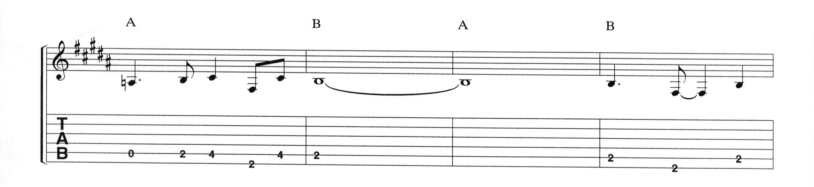

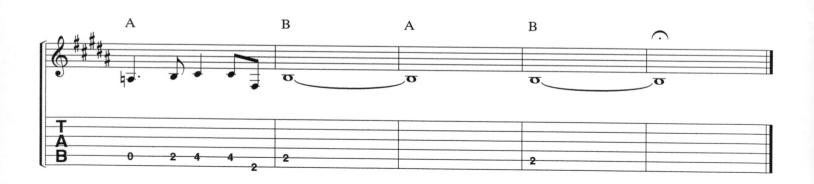

WALKING ALONE

Lyrics by BILLIE JOE
Music by BILLIE JOE and GREEN DAY

Verse:

1. Come to- geth- er like a foot in a shoe,____ on- ly
2. Walk on egg- shells on my old stomp- ing ground,____

this time I think I stuck my foot in my mouth.____
yet there's real- ly no one left that's hang- ing a- round.

Think- ing out____ loud and act- ing in vain,____
Is- n't that an- oth- er fa- mil- iar face?____

knock- ing o- ver an- y- one that stands in my way.____
Too drunk to fig- ure out they're fad- ing a- way.____ }

Walking Alone - 3 - 1
0224B

JINX

Lyrics by BILLIE JOE
Music by BILLIE JOE and GREEN DAY

Jinx - 4 - 1
0224B

62

Interlude:

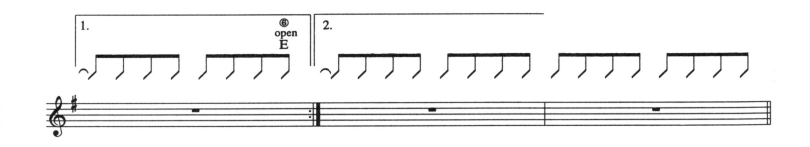

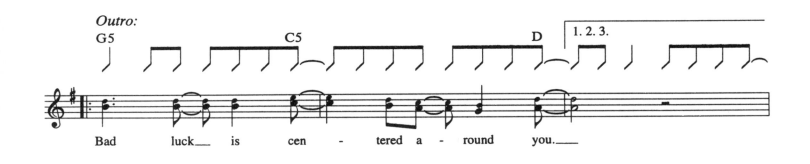

Outro:

Bad luck___ is cen - tered a - round you.___

Segue to Haushinka

HAUSHINKA

Lyrics by BILLIE JOE
Music by BILLIE JOE and GREEN DAY

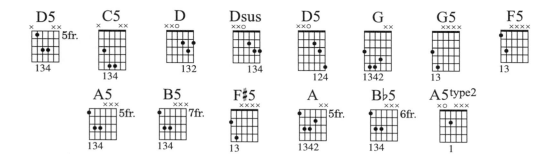

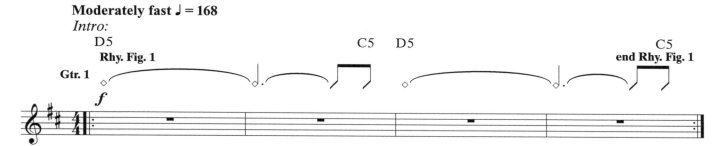

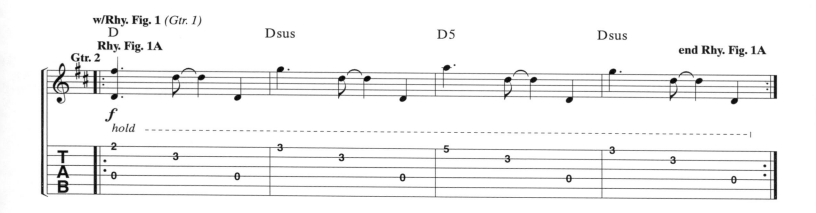

Haushinka - 4 - 1
0224B

66

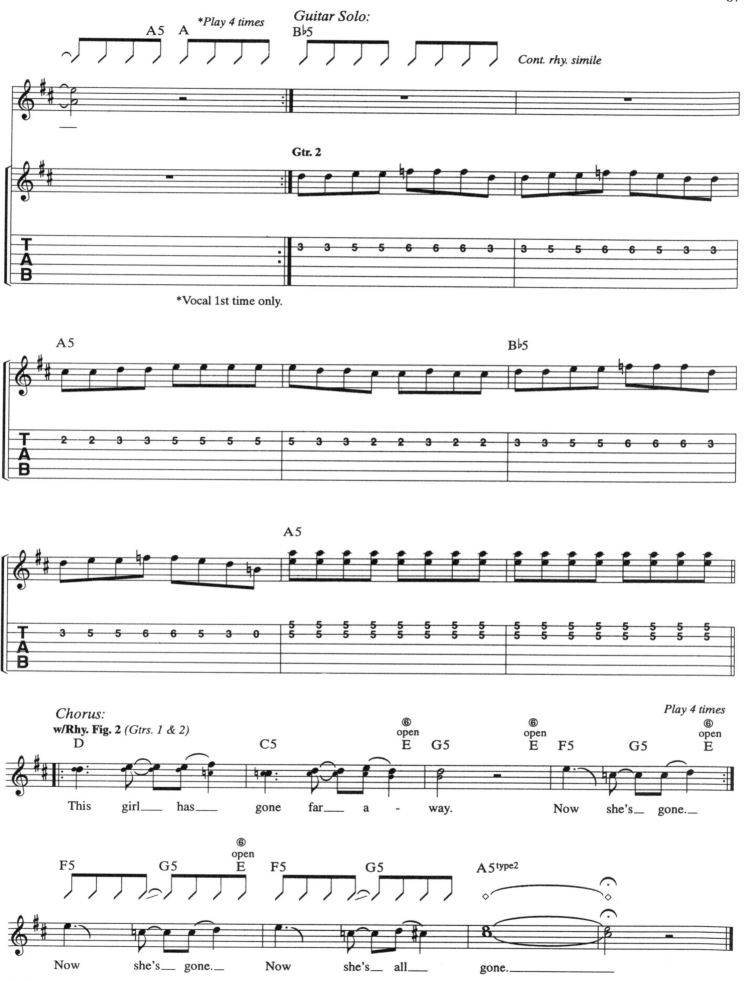

REJECT

Lyrics by BILLIE JOE
Music by BILLIE JOE and GREEN DAY

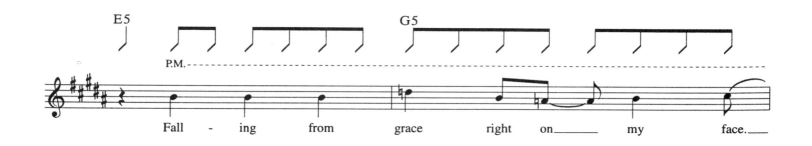

Fall - ing from grace right on____ my face.____

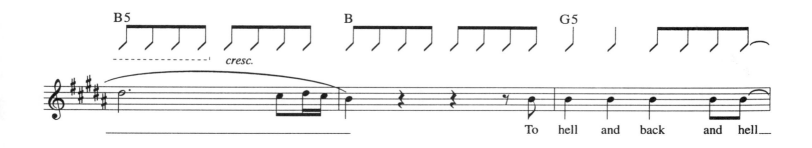

To hell and back and hell____

____ a - gain,__ I've gone.

TAKE BACK

Lyrics by BILLIE JOE
Music by BILLIE JOE and GREEN DAY

Tune down 1/2 step:

⑥ = E♭   ③ = G♭
⑤ = A♭   ② = B♭
④ = D♭   ① = E♭

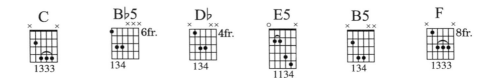

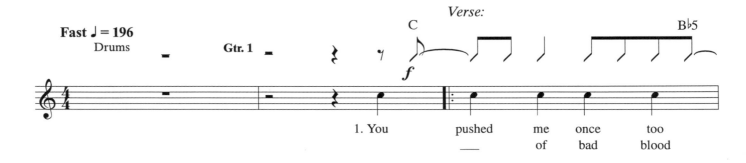

1. You pushed me once too
   ___ of bad blood

far a-gain,___ I'd love___ to break your fuck-ing teeth,___ I'd stick
on *the* tip___ of my tongue. An eye for an eye, a gun for___ a gun.___

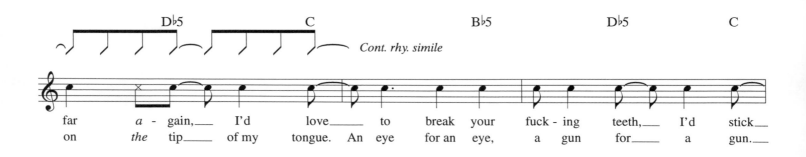

___ a knife in the cen-ter of___ your back.___
___ Cold-cocked, I'm tak-ing back___ what's mine.___

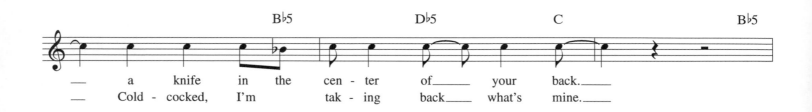

You bet-ter grow some eyes___ in the back of your head.___
Ex-pect___ it when your least___ ex-pect-ing it.___

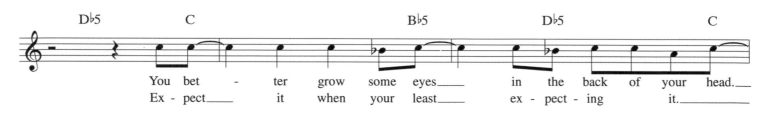

Take Back - 2 - 1
0224B

KING FOR A DAY

Lyrics by BILLIE JOE
Music by BILLIE JOE and GREEN DAY

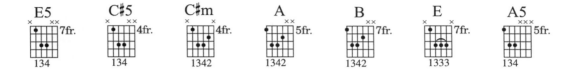

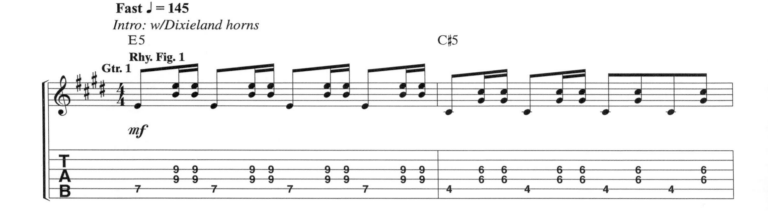

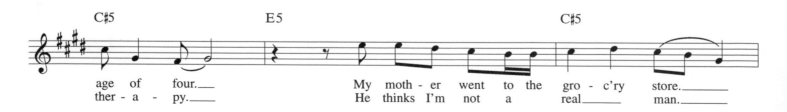

King for a Day - 5 - 1
0224B

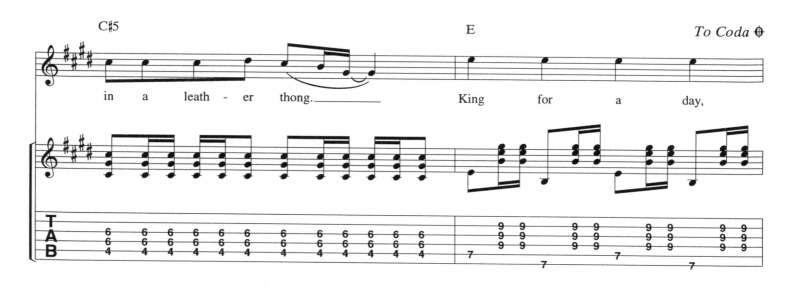

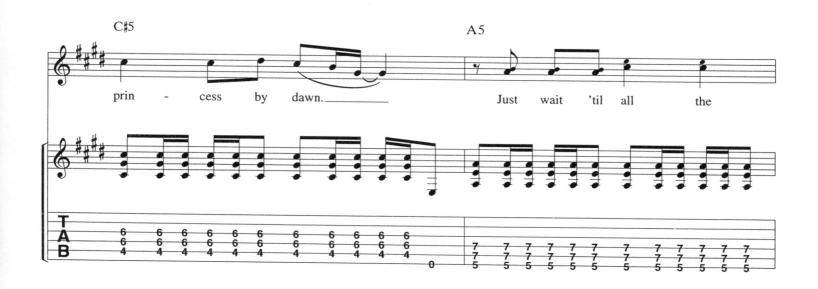

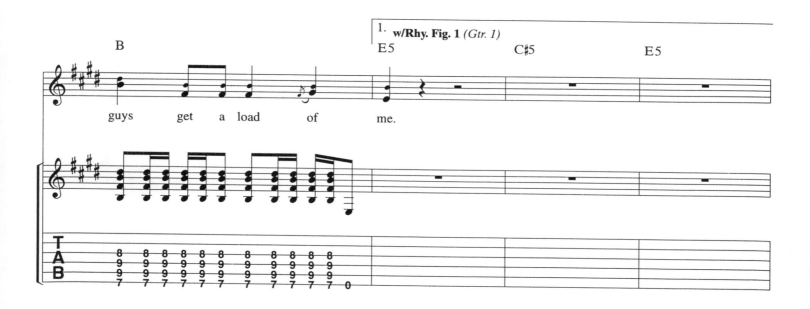

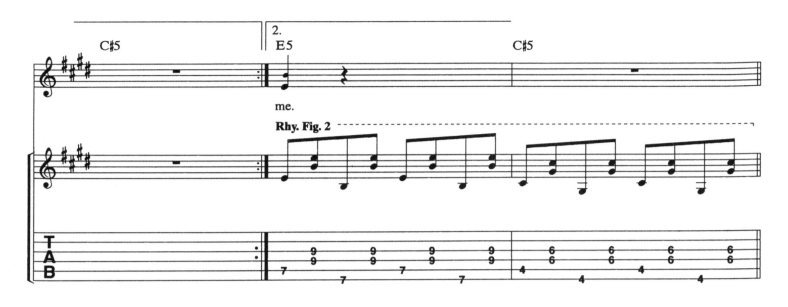

Interlude: w/Dixieland horns

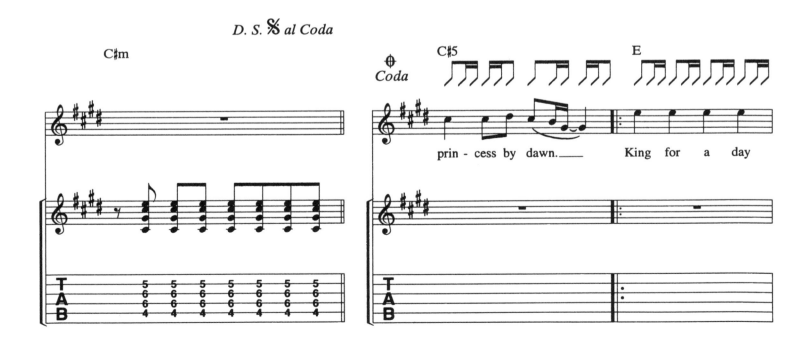

Outro: w/Dixieland horns

GOOD RIDDANCE (TIME OF YOUR LIFE)

Lyrics by BILLIE JOE
Music by BILLIE JOE and GREEN DAY

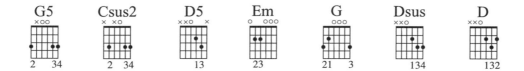

Fast ♩ = 172
Intro:
G5

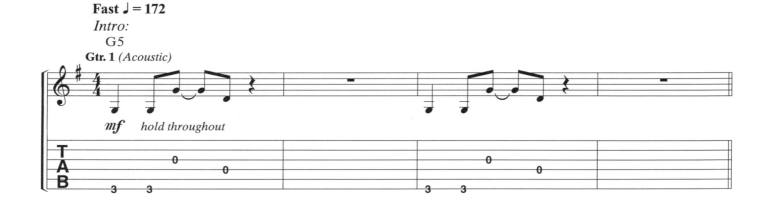

Verse:
G5
Gtr. 1 cont. rhy. simile

1. An - oth - er turn - ing point, a fork
2. So take the pho - to - graphs and still - frames

Good Riddance (Time of Your Life) - 3 - 1
0224B

PROSTHETIC HEAD

Lyrics by BILLIE JOE
Music by BILLIE JOE and GREEN DAY

Prosthetic Head - 4 - 1
0224B

84

GUITAR TAB GLOSSARY **

TABLATURE EXPLANATION

READING TABLATURE: Tablature illustrates the six strings of the guitar. Notes and chords are indicated by the placement of fret numbers on a given string(s).

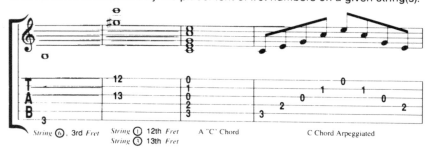

String ⑥, 3rd *Fret*   String ① 12th *Fret*   A "C" Chord   C Chord Arpeggiated
String ③ 13th *Fret*

BENDING NOTES

HALF STEP: Play the note and bend string one half step.*

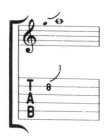

WHOLE STEP: Play the note and bend string one whole step.

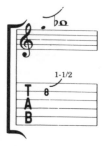

WHOLE STEP AND A HALF: Play the note and bend string a whole step and a half.

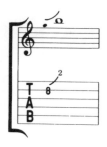

TWO STEPS: Play the note and bend string two whole steps.

SLIGHT BEND (Microtone): Play the note and bend string slightly to the equivalent of half a fret.

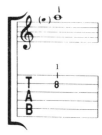

PREBEND (Ghost Bend): Bend to the specified note, before the string is picked.

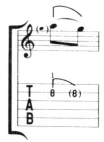

PREBEND AND RELEASE: Bend the string, play it, then release to the original note.

REVERSE BEND: Play the already-bent string, then immediately drop it down to the fretted note.

BEND AND RELEASE: Play the note and gradually bend to the next pitch, then release to the original note. Only the first note is attacked.

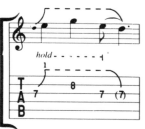

BENDS INVOLVING MORE THAN ONE STRING: Play the note and bend string while playing an additional note (or notes) on another string(s). Upon release, relieve pressure from additional note(s), causing original note to sound alone.

BENDS INVOLVING STATIONARY NOTES: Play notes and bend lower pitch, then hold until release begins (indicated at the point where line becomes solid).

UNISON BEND: Play both notes and immediately bend the lower note to the same pitch as the higher note.

DOUBLE NOTE BEND: Play both notes and immediately bend both strings simultaneously.

*A half step is the smallest interval in Western music; it is equal to one fret. A whole step equals two frets.

© 1990 Beam Me Up Music
c/o CPP/Belwin, Inc. Miami, Florida 33014
International Copyright Secured   Made in U.S.A.   All Rights Reserved   **By Kenn Chipkin and Aaron Stang

RHYTHM SLASHES

STRUM INDICATIONS: Strum with indicated rhythm.

The chord voicings are found on the first page of the transcription underneath the song title.

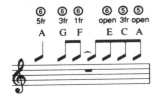

INDICATING SINGLE NOTES USING RHYTHM SLASHES: Very often single notes are incorporated into a rhythm part. The note name is indicated above the rhythm slash with a fret number and a string indication.

ARTICULATIONS

HAMMER ON: Play lower note, then "hammer on" to higher note with another finger. Only the first note is attacked.

LEFT HAND HAMMER: Hammer on the first note played on each string with the left hand.

PULL OFF: Play higher note, then "pull off" to lower note with another finger. Only the first note is attacked.

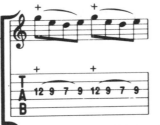

FRETBOARD TAPPING: "Tap" onto the note indicated by + with a finger of the pick hand, then pull off to the following note held by the fret hand.

TAP SLIDE: Same as fretboard tapping, but the tapped note is slid randomly up the fretboard, then pulled off to the following note.

BEND AND TAP TECHNIQUE: Play note and bend to specified interval. While holding bend, tap onto note indicated.

LEGATO SLIDE: Play note and slide to the following note. (Only first note is attacked).

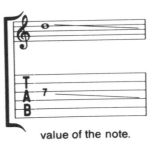

LONG GLISSANDO: Play note and slide in specified direction for the full value of the note.

SHORT GLISSANDO: Play note for its full value and slide in specified direction at the last possible moment.

PICK SLIDE: Slide the edge of the pick in specified direction across the length of the string(s).

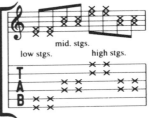

MUTED STRINGS: A percussive sound is made by laying the fret hand across all six strings while pick hand strikes specified area (low, mid, high strings).

PALM MUTE: The note or notes are muted by the palm of the pick hand by lightly touching the string(s) near the bridge.

TREMOLO PICKING: The note or notes are picked as fast as possible.

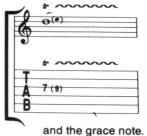

TRILL: Hammer on and pull off consecutively and as fast as possible between the original note and the grace note.

ACCENT: Notes or chords are to be played with added emphasis.

STACCATO (Detached Notes): Notes or chords are to be played roughly half their actual value and with separation.

DOWN STROKES AND UPSTROKES: Notes or chords are to be played with either a downstroke (⊓ ·) or upstroke (∨) of the pick.

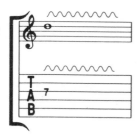

VIBRATO: The pitch of a note is varied by a rapid shaking of the fret hand finger, wrist, and forearm.

HARMONICS

NATURAL HARMONIC: A finger of the fret hand lightly touches the note or notes indicated in the tab and is played by the pick hand.

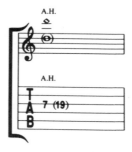

ARTIFICIAL HARMONIC: The first tab number is fretted, then the pick hand produces the harmonic by using a finger to lightly touch the same string at the second tab number (in parenthesis) and is then picked by another finger.

ARTIFICIAL "PINCH" HARMONIC: A note is fretted as indicated by the tab, then the pick hand produces the harmonic by squeezing the pick firmly while using the tip of the index finger in the pick attack. If parenthesis are found around the fretted note, it does not sound. No parenthesis means both the fretted note and A.H. are heard simultaneously.

TREMOLO BAR

SPECIFIED INTERVAL: The pitch of a note or chord is lowered to a specified interval and then may or may not return to the original pitch. The activity of the tremolo bar is graphically represented by peaks and valleys.

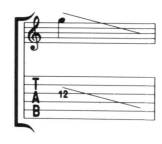

UNSPECIFIED INTERVAL: The pitch of a note or a chord is lowered to an unspecified interval.